The North

The North

Sherman Hines

Foreword by Fred Bruemmer

NIMBUS PUBLISHING LIMITED

To the memory of my father, Vernon O.
Hines. Without his teachings of hunting and
survival skills during my formative years,
this book would not have been possible.

Nimbus Publishing Limited
P.O. Box 9301, Station A
Halifax, Nova Scotia
B3K 5N5

Canadian Cataloguing in Publication Data

Hines, Sherman, 1941–

   The North
   ISBN 0-921054-33-5

1. Canada, Northern — Description and travel — Views.
I. Title.

FC3956.H46 1990   971.9'0022'2   C90-097506-7
F1090.5.H46 1990

Printed and bound in Hong Kong
by Everbest Printing Co., Ltd.

Cover: Iceberg, Cumberland Sound, Northwest Territories.

Page 2, Back Cover: David Tucktoo, Inuk hunter from Spence Bay, Boothia
Peninsula, Northwest Territories.

Right: Bearberry and dwarf willow in fall colours near Tombstone River
along the Dempster Highway, Yukon.

Foreword

The North. Its sheer immensity is awesome. The Northwest Territories and the Yukon cover nearly half of Canada yet have a combined population of only 65 000, one person to every 27 square miles. Great Bear Lake is bigger than Belgium, and Ellesmere Island, nearly the size of Great Britain, has a population of 89. The North is a vast and empty land, the largest wilderness on earth. It is a strangely haunting land: the dark, spired forest, the flaming birches of fall, the endless rolling tundra, the myriad nameless lakes, the loneliness, the infinite space. Some love it and some fear it, but it is a land that few ever forget.

It is such a contradictory land, new yet ancient, harsh and rugged yet oddly fragile, terribly poor yet incredibly rich.

Nearly all of it is new land. It emerged only about 8 000 years ago from beneath the mile-thick ice sheets that had covered it for more than 1000 centuries. It is a naked, riven land, indelibly marked by the grinding ice, its gashes and wounds thinly mantled by vegetation. Great mounds of lichen-covered stones mark glacial moraines. Snow buntings often nest in these ancient rock piles, and lithe, deadly weasels make them their home. Eskers, the compacted sediment of sub-glacial rivers, meander across the tundra like misplaced embankments, their sandy soil the best denning place for arctic foxes and wolves. Erratics litter the land, boulders sheared from mountains and ridges by the passing ice, carried along and dumped on the plains. Owls and hawks like to perch on them, and they are often covered with vivid lichens. In this nitrogen-poor land, every bit of fertilizer attracts grateful plants.

To us from the south, it is a new land also in a different sense. When J.W. Tyrrell of the Canadian Geological Survey crossed in 1893 that ". . . great mysterious region of *terra incognita* commonly known as the Barren Lands . . ." (an area much larger than France), ". . . of almost this entire territory less was known than of the remotest districts of 'Darkest Africa'." Henry Hudson sailed into Hudson Bay in 1610, but many of the islands in northern Foxe Basin were not discovered and named until the late 1930s. Prince Leopold Island was briefly seen and named by the explorer William Parry in 1819. But that this island is home to one of the most spectacular seabird colonies in Canada was only discovered in 1958 by Dr. Thomas W. Barry of the Canadian Wildlife Service.

And yet it is an ancient land. On a high beach overlooking a seal-rich, rock-girt bay on southern Baffin Island, the archeologist Dr. Moreau S. Maxwell has for many years dug down patiently through many layers of human habitation. Upon this remote and lonely spot, he found, Inuit and their ancestors had lived continuously, generation upon generation, for more than 4 000 years. Long before Vancouver was discovered, Toronto was dreamt of, or Montreal was founded, Elizabethan sailors and miners camped on Baffin Island, in 1577, and had many a row with the natives, who, says a contemporary account, shot their ". . . General in the Buttocke with an arrow . . ." That "General" was Martin Frobisher, moiling for gold on an islet called Kodlunarn by the Inuit, "the island of white men", and still marked by broad trenches where they dug out the ore.

It is a rich land hemmed by an even richer sea. Each summer more than 1000 white whales swim into Somerset Island's Cunningham Inlet. They surge through the cool, green, pellucid water like gleaming ivory-white torpedoes, their heart-shaped flukes rising and falling in smooth cadence, glittering bow waves curling against their bluff-browed heads. Hundreds of walruses sleep huddled together on broad beaches of Coats Island in Hudson Bay, and hundreds of thousands of murres breed on the sheer cliffs of Digges Islands and Cape Wolstenholme, where Hudson Strait turns into Hudson Bay. One long-ago summer, I lived with an Inuk family at the narrows between Aberdeen and Beverly lakes in the central Barrens. Here, since time immemorial, caribou have crossed and Inuit have waited for them. A few came first, a scattered, ambling vanguard, and then came the drawn out herds, an urgent throng driven by the ancient instinct of migration, a grey-brown river of life that flowed past our camp for three days and four nights.

Such animal concentrations are temporary and local, for the land, in truth, is poor and fragile. That is why the caribou, the last of the great wildlife herds of this continent, wander forever to reach new pastures. Plant productivity in the North is only about 1 per cent of that of southern lands. The dense cushion of mountain avens gaily spangled with white and gold blooms may be 100–200 years old. A patch of lichen no larger than your palm took 1000 years to attain this size. Cart tracks made on Melville Island by Parry's 1819–1820 expedition remain clearly visible, and no lichens touch as yet the florid signature the explorer Samuel Hearne scratched into rock near Churchill, Manitoba, on "July $\overset{e}{y}$ 1, 1767".

Nearly all Inuit now live in towns and settlements, in houses much like those in the south. They are hunters, artists, miners, teachers, trappers, oil drillers or administrators. Come spring and the end of the school year, an odd restlessness pervades northern villages. The people return to the land. They camp again near the bays and the rivers where their ancestors caught seal and speared char and renew again that nearly mystical bond that ties them to this austere yet magnificent land.

Fred Bruemmer

Overleaf: Iceberg, Cumberland Sound, Northwest Territories.

Red currants, Yukon.

Red-capped soldier lichen, Yukon.

Outfitter and guide for canoe and dog-team wilderness trips Bruce Johnson and daughter Bronwyn, Atlin River, British Columbia.

Left: Sunset at Taku, Graham Inlet, British Columbia.

Ogilvie Mountains near where the Blackstone River crosses the Dempster Highway, Yukon.

Left: Aspen along the Klondike Highway, Yukon.

Overleaf: The advancing face of the Llewellyn Glacier from the icecap in the boundary range of the Coast Mountains, British Columbia.

An Indian of the Loucheux Tribe at his camp, south of Fort McPherson, Northwest Territories.

Right: Moose-hunting camp of the Loucheux Indians, north of Eagle Plains and Rock River, Yukon.

The village of Nain, Labrador, in a snowstorm.

Jocko, Inuk from the northern-most village in Labrador: Nain.

Overflow on the east Blackstone River along the Dempster Highway, Yukon.

Right: Near Eagle Plains on the Dempster Highway, Yukon.

Overleaf: Children cutting wood in a blizzard, Nain, Labrador.

Top: Ungava Bay at Kuujjuaq (Fort-Chimo), Quebec.
Bottom: Airport at Kuujjuaq (Fort-Chimo), Quebec.

Right: Cumberland Sound, Northwest Territories.

Arctic cotton grass, Pond Inlet, Northwest Territories.

Canada jays backlit on a frosty morning.

The Penny Ice Cap, Auyuittuq National Park, Cumberland Peninsula, Baffin Island, Northwest Territories.

Richardson Mountains, Yukon.

Rest period for a dog, Spence Bay, Northwest Territories.

Strong wind and blowing snow, Nain, Labrador.

Lichen, moss and mushrooms, Yukon–British Columbia border.

Right: Rosehip, an important source of vitamin C.

Squirrel-tail grass along the Dempster Highway, Yukon.

Right: Arctic ground squirrel, Yukon.

Looking north across Pond Inlet, Baffin Island, Northwest Territories.

Right: Packhorse, Weir Mountain, British Columbia.

Overleaf: Iceberg in Cumberland Sound, off the mount of Pangnirtung Fiord, Northwest Territories.

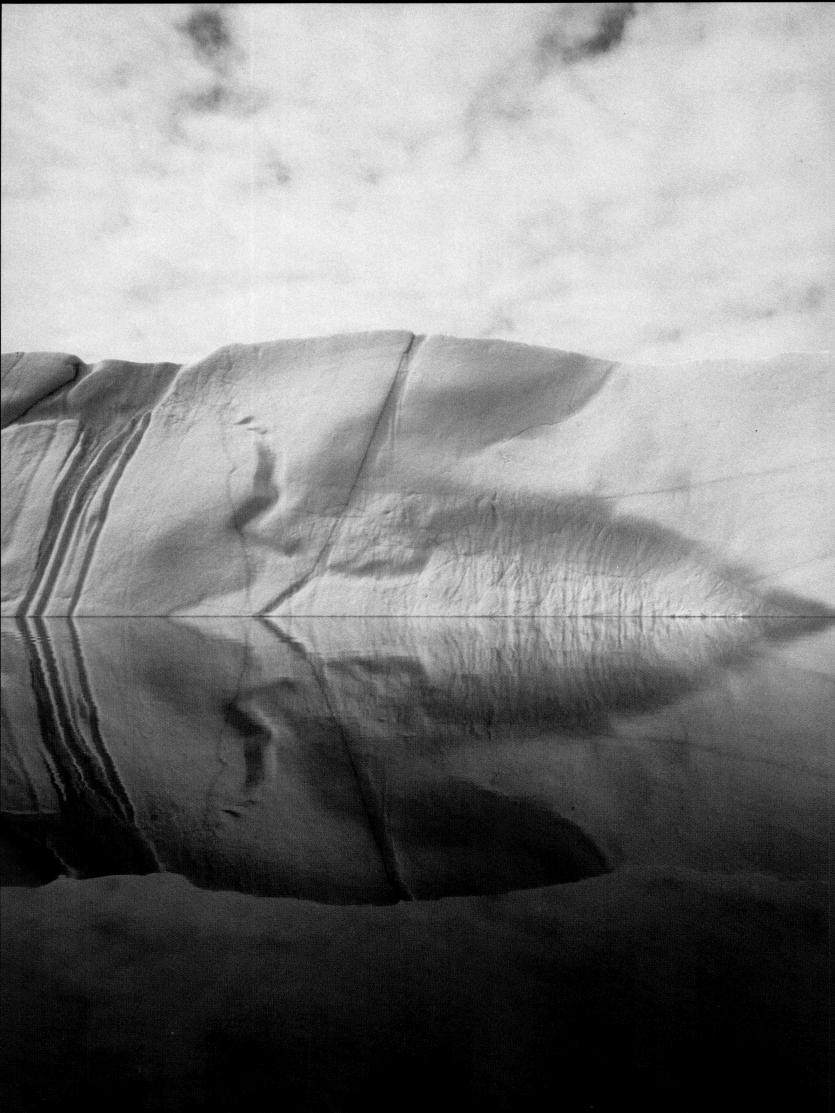

Polar bear stalking quarry, Hudson Bay.

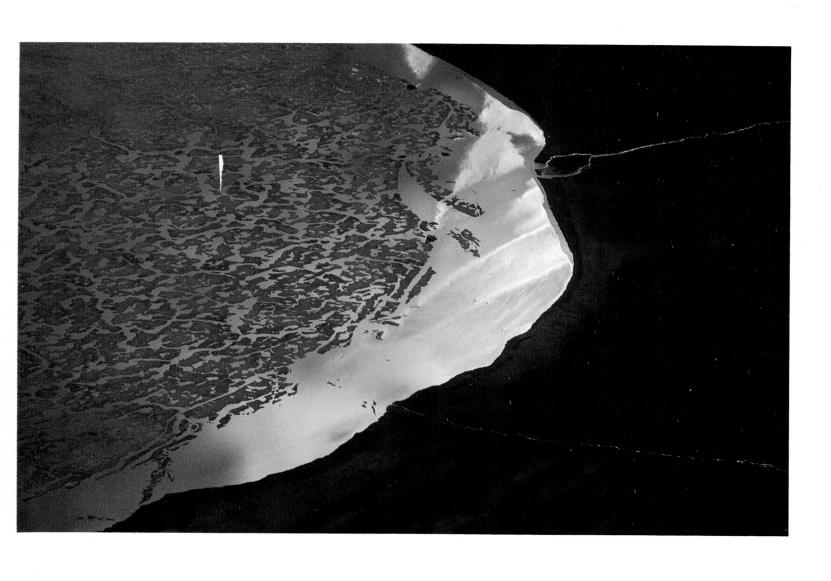

Lancaster Sound from the air. Spring ice creates an interesting pattern, Northwest Territories.

Pangnirtung Fiord, the Pangnirtung entrance to Auyuittuq National Park, Northwest Territories.

Left: Ross Peyton, innkeeper, fishing guide, Peyton Inn, Pangnirtung, Northwest Territories.

Children of Pelly Bay, Simpson Peninsula, Northwest Territories.

Right: Taku, British Columbia, near Yukon border.

McIntyre Creek, Klondike Highway, north of Whitehorse, Yukon.

Lunch on the trail with dog-team outfitter Bruce Johnson, Atlin, British Columbia.

Dwarf birch, aspen, bearberry and lichen add colour to the fall scenery along the
Dempster Highway, Yukon.

Right: Arctic poppies, Pond Inlet, Northwest Territories.

Cape Dorset, Fox Peninsula, Baffin Island, Northwest Territories.

Getting a ride in the *amutik*, Pangnirtung, Northwest Territories.

Inuit families en route to fishing and hunting camps near Thom Bay, Boothia Peninsula, Northwest Territories.

Right: Inuk hunter, Spence Bay, Boothia Peninsula, Northwest Territories.

Overleaf: Blackstone River in the heart of the Ogilvie Mountains, Yukon.

Ken Whitmire, ready to drop the snow anchor, Atlin Lake with Hitchcock
Mountain in background, British Columbia.

Right: Off the Dempster Highway, Yukon.

Inuk hunter David Tucktoo, in camouflage for hunting on the ice, Thom Bay, Boothia Peninsula, Northwest Territories.

Left: Inuk soapstone carver from Spence Bay, Northwest Territories.

Frost-covered bush near Bar C, between Inuvik and Tuktoyaktuk, Northwest Territories.

Left: Sunlight and shadows, Richardson Mountains, Yukon.

Dick Smith, hunter guide and outfitter, with the Tintern Mountains and Fox
Creek Valley in background, British Columbia.

Tombstone Mountain Valley from the Dempster Highway, Yukon.

Dawson, Yukon, heart of the Gold Rush of 1898.

Left: Cross-country skiing, Atlin Lake, British Columbia.

Engineer Creek, in the Richardson Mountains, Yukon.

The Ogilvie Mountains and the Blackstone River, Yukon.

Klondike River at Rock Creek, near Dawson, Yukon.

Klondike River near Rock Creek, −50°C, Yukon.

Overleaf: Camping in the valley of the Weasel River, Auyuittuq National Park, Cumberland Peninsula, Baffin Island, Northwest Territories.

Rainstorm over the Terrahina Creek, near Weir Mountain, British Columbia.

Right: Inuit with cargo canoe, Cumberland Sound, Pangnirtung, Northwest Territories.

Near Chapman Lake and the Dempster Highway, Yukon.

5 550' peak at the North Fork Pass, on the Dempster Highway, Yukon.

Fungus, Atlin Lake, British Columbia.

Pine cones, needles, lichen and twigs at the 12-Kilometre Camp, Atlin Lake, British Columbia.

Overleaf: Taku, where the Atlin River enters Graham Inlet, British Columbia, with Table Mountain in background.

Hiking along the Weasel River flats, Auyuittuq National Park, Pangnirtung,
Northwest Territories.

Mountains of the boundary range near the Llewellyn Glacier at the south end of Atlin Lake, British Columbia.

Fishing at Antler Bay, Atlin Lake, British Columbia.

Right: Trout fishing on Antler Bay, Atlin Lake, British Columbia.

Ruffed grouse, Yukon.

Right: Lichen growth is very slow in the Arctic climate; some species are
between 25 and 100 years of age. Yukon.

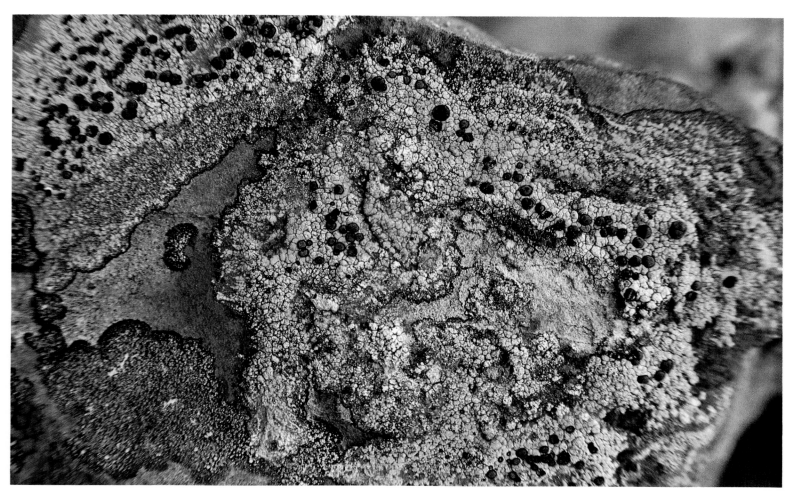

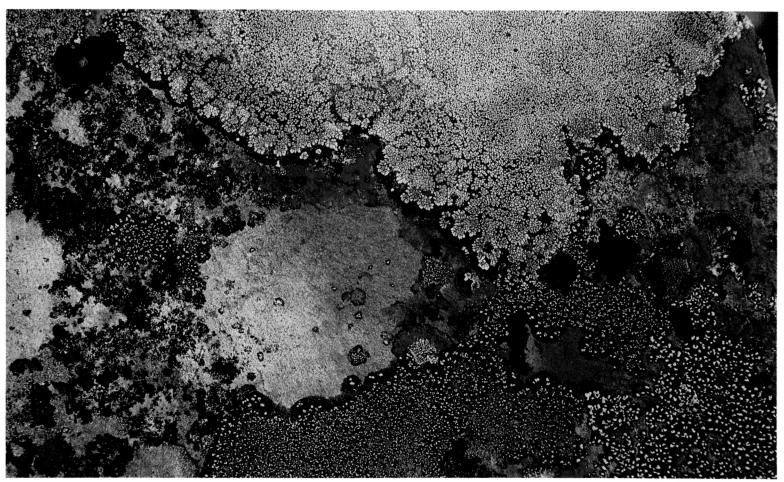

Overleaf: Pangnirtung Fiord, Baffin Island, Northwest Territories.

Travelling by snow machine and *kamotik* near Spence Bay, Northwest Territories.

Left, upper: Frobisher Bay.
Lower: Tuktoyaktuk, Northwest Territories.

Iceberg, Cumberland Sound, Northwest Territories.

Left: Polar bears around Hudson Bay.

Cumberland Sound, Northwest Territories.

Yellowknife, on Great Slave Lake, Northwest Territories.

Approaching Antler Bay near Griffith Island, Atlin Lake, British Columbia.

Spring break-up of ice with snow crystals.

Looking over Fox Creek Valley, Tintern Mountains, British Columbia.

Left: Coronation Fiord, Baffin Island, Northwest Territories.

Limestone used in the printmaking process, Cape Dorset, Northwest Territories.

Left: Inuit artist, Cape Dorset, Northwest Territories.

Hailstone cones and leaves create an interesting pattern.

Willow ptarmigan, Eagle Plains, Yukon.

Overleaf: Iceberg, Cumberland Sound, Northwest Territories.

Rock formations around Hudson Bay near Churchill, Manitoba.

Right: Nanuk, the Inuit name for polar bear. Waiting for Hudson Bay to freeze over.

McIntyre Creek, north of Whitehorse, Yukon.

Rock and willow ptarmigan in winter plumage.

Ice formations created by changes in water levels in the Atlin River, British Columbia.

Clusters of frost crystals on ice near Dawson, Yukon.

Overleaf: Musk oxen in loose defence ring, Polar Bear Pass, Bathurst Island,
Northwest Territories.

Trucking through the Ogilvie Mountains on the Dempster Highway, Yukon.

Seemingly endless road through the Richardson Mountains along the
Dempster Highway, Yukon.

Late-afternoon light on the tundra near the Antimony Mountains.

Left: Fireweed, Yukon.

Pangnirtung, population 905, Baffin Island, Northwest Territories.

Left: Cargo canoe returning from spring camp near Pangnirtung, Baffin Island, Northwest Territories.

Overleaf: One of dozens of glaciers flowing from the Penny Ice Cap, Baffin Island, Northwest Territories.

Arctic hare. Eureka. Ellesmere Island, Northwest Territories.

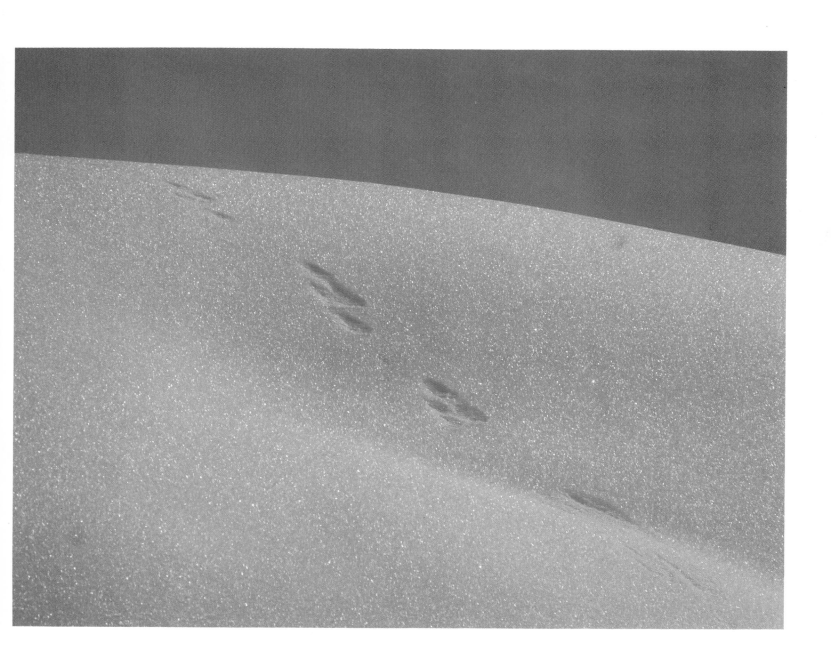

Arctic-hare tracks, Northwest Territories.

Snow covering bushes along the Klondike Highway, Yukon.

Dwarf arctic willow, Auyuittuq National Park, Northwest Territories.

Ogilvie Mountains, Yukon.

Left: Broad-leaved willow herb, Auyuittuq National Park, Northwest Territories.

Mount Minto, north end of Atlin Lake, British Columbia.

Right: Annie Gordon, Kuujjuaq (Fort-Chimo), Quebec.

Packhorses in the Tintern Mountains, British Columbia.

Right: Dick and Holly Smith, guides and outfitters, Indian River Ranch, Atlin, British Columbia.

Sundogs, Arctic Red River, Northwest Territories.

Left: Tuktoyaktuk, Beaufort Sea, Northwest Territories.

Riverboat *Klondike*, Whitehorse, Yukon.

Right: Frobisher Bay, Baffin Island, Northwest Territories.

Overleaf: An igloo made by cutting blocks of hard snow.

Snowdrift near Nain, Labrador.

Fox tracks packed hard and then windswept, Thom Bay, near Spence Bay, Northwest Territories.

Dempster Highway, Yukon.

Iceberg, Cumberland Sound, Northwest Territories.

Fishing for pike. Eva Lake, south of the Yukon–British Columbia border.

Atlin, Atlin Lake, British Columbia, south of Whitehorse, Yukon.

Curious polar bear along the coast of Hudson Bay, Churchill, Manitoba.

Grise Fiord, Ellesmere Island, Northwest Territories.

Fall colours along the Dempster Highway, Yukon.

Left: Bob Fraser, prospector, cook and guide, Atlin, British Columbia.

Mare's-tail, Atlin Lake, British Columbia.

Snow crystals on ice in a shallow brook, Yukon.

Waiting for the six-metre tide, Pangnirtung, Northwest Territories.

Right: Inuit outfitter, Pangnirtung, Northwest Territories.

Overleaf: Dog teams crossing Atlin Lake with Birch Mountain, Teresa Island, in background, British Columbia.

Ice formations, Atlin River, British Columbia.

Right: Sap of a spruce tree, running out of the breaks in the bark caused by bear claws.

Along the Dempster Highway, Richardson Mountains, Yukon.

Snow detail along the Dempster Highway, Yukon.

Caribou camp Bull Creek, near Red Mountain, British Columbia.

Mountain caribou on the crest of Red Mountain, British Columbia.

Special thanks to
Dick Smith, Bruce
Johnson, David Tucktoo

All book photographs available from
Masterfile Stock Photo Library
415 Yonge Street
Suite 200
Toronto, Canada
1-416-977-7267
1-800-387-9010

Cameras: Pentax 6 × 7
and Contax with Carl Zeiss T. lens
Film: Fujichrome